The Inner Me

Rownan Christophers

The Inner Me

Acknowledgements

There are two people to whom I am indebted: firstly, my good long-time friend and mentor, creative writing teacher and now artist, Eric Payne, who was more than happy to allow me to use one of a multitude of his pictures for the cover page of this, my first publication. To see a full array of his gallery, go to www.ericpayneartist@hotmail.com.au or look him up on Facebook at contact@ericpayne.com.au

My second and equally important acknowledgement goes to Stephen Matthews, my publisher at Ginninderra Press, for allowing me the freedom to use Eric's cover image.

Many, many thanks, gentlemen!

The Inner Me
ISBN 978 1 76041 296 8
Copyright © text Rownan Christophers 2017
Cover image: Eric Payne, *Moonlight at Maligne Bay*

First published 2017 by
GINNINDERRA PRESS
PO Box 3461 Port Adelaide 5015
www.ginninderrapress.com.au

Contents

Dedications	7
Foreword	9
Zelma	11
The River of Love	12
Sunset and Us	13
The Last Time I Saw Him	14
Our Special Place	16
A Winter's Day	17
South Africa	18
Autumn	19
Winter	20
Spring	21
Summer	22
White Wings at Dawn	23
The Steely Bear	24
The Ghost of Emptiness	25
Cold and Alone	26
Somewhere In My Head	28
Waterside Heaven	30
The Sound of Death	31
Endless Night	32
Goodbye My Little Friend	34
The Longest Trek	36
Don't Mourn for Me	37
It's Never Easy	38
Into the Darkness	39
The Detour	40
Another New Chapter	42
The Seed	43
You Are the Candle	44

One Candle	45
Side By Side	46
The Tears You Cry	47
Not Once	48
Only For You	49
Power of the Rose	50
My Angel	51
The Circle	52
The Ruins	53
A House Is Like a Baby	54
A Pleasant Place	55
Candlelight Dancer	56
Eric	57
Jude	58

Dedications

This, my first book of poems, is dedicated to a number of people. To my daughters: Lorraine, Louise Stephanie and Rebecca and their respective families. It is also dedicated to my long-time friends, Mark and Lorraine Allen, and to four other very important people in my life who believed in me as a writer. They are my lovely and devoted wife, Zelma, for whom many of these poems were written; Sue Fleming, my TAFESA coordinator ('The Steely Bear'); and Eric Payne, a former teacher as well as a friend and mentor, a man to whom I owe so much. He not only taught me so much about myself as a writer, he believed in my abilities as a writer. Eric gave me a gift or, if you'd like to put it another way, a tool for my writer's toolbox – the faith and willingness to accept helpful criticism which, in turn, made me a better writer than I already was – and it was during my time in Creative Writing with him that I wrote 'The Sound of Death'. He also gave me another snippet of useful information: 'You've got to love what you're writing or there's no point in starting to write [it].'

These dedications would not be complete, however, unless I mentioned the wonderful and gifted Jude Aquilina, a published poet in her own right. Jude was my TAFE mentor in this project and responsible for me writing 'The Last Time I Saw Him', along with a few others in this collection. She, too, has become a friend of mine and somebody that I honestly respect.

A good friend once said to me, 'You're the only bloke I know who could make a person's flesh crawl with the stories you write and yet you can reduce a person to a teary-eyed blubbering mess with your poetry.' So here you go, Tony T, read and weep, my long-time friend.

Finally, in closing, this little collection is also for all of those friends, both students and staff, that I made during my time at Para West and TAFESA. Thanks for the memories, guys.

Foreword

I have been writing poetry on and off for over forty years and this collection includes only a small portion of the poems I have written.

Influences over the years have come from different sources, such as people, including my lovely, loyal and very patient wife, Zelma. Animals have also contributed in one way or another to what I write, as have music, nature and death, morbid as it sounds.

Poetry allows me to bare a portion of my heart and soul to you, the reader, and my only hope is that you enjoy what you read and are touched by it in some way.

Zelma

Zealous is the word that describes you and your love best
Ecstatic, delightful and joyful…a true rapture in human form
Loving and loyal, a woman to behold
Mother and grandmother of many and matriarch of the clan
Assertive and affectionate to the core.

The River of Love

The river flows on by
slowly, quietly and lazily under a moonlit sky.
Small wavelets lap gently at the banks
while clouds dance on by.
In the emptiness of the evening sky
we lie on a blanket in each other's arms
listening to the sounds around us
and just as pure is this
piece of nature,
so is our love.

Sunset and Us

We are alone, far removed from
the world we left behind,
the constant grind, grind, grind.

We're here alone absorbing all of the magic,
all of the beauty of the sunset.
And just like the glory of the skyline,
there's no end to our love.

The Last Time I Saw Him

It's been many a year
since I last saw him
high up in the mountains
far from here,
up Mount Wellington way,
from memory.

His hair, white and shoulder length,
was stiff like knotted wire,
a real tangled mess;
his teeth – what there was of them –
were an ugly shade of black and decayed
truly – a dentist's nightmare.

He had long, slender and dirty fingers
with nails that badly needed cutting
for they were more like an eagle's talons.

His shirt – what was left of it –
was like his teeth, dirty and just as holey;
his trousers were held up by string,
and quite odorous, to be polite,
for they were soiled beyond belief
and stank to the highest height.

With a voice that was low and raspy,
and his speech, although limited,
was far from audible –
more like a pig's grunts.

To shake his hand was quite a task,
for it was like gripping a felled tree;
it'd rasp the flesh from your hands,
if you tried to pull away.

I haven't seen him since that time.
I can't tell you where he'd be these days
or even if he's still alive.

Our Special Place

Here in our hideaway
far from prying eyes we live
and play, just you and I,
sharing all the magical beauty that
Mother Nature has provided.

Dense forests, waterfalls and rock pools,
birds and creatures of every kind,
even a monkey or two:
these are the things that make up our Utopia,
just us and us alone.

Burnt-orange sunsets and balmy winds bid the day goodbye
and bright pearly-white moons are our night light.
Lazy waves in the distance lap the shore
like a rhythmic nursery rhyme.
All of this and so much more
in this, our special place.

A Winter's Day

On a rainswept street in a little hamlet
we walk along together arm in arm under
the shelter of an umbrella, blending in
without talking to any who may pass us by.

The rain falls harder and it's colder,
so much colder, we huddle closer
together as we make our way home
to an open fireplace where logs are blazing;
it beckons and warms us.

We sit in silence on the soft white rug
sipping freshly made hot chocolate
with marshmallows and cuddle close together.
Sweet, sweet beautiful winter,
how we love it,
and each other.

South Africa

So here I am at last,
On safari, trekking in a land so wild and free,
Ultimately astounded by all that I see,
Taking all of it in and
Happy to be, living the dream,
A world of raw, untamed beauty,
Far from anything I have ever known,
Rich in diversity and wild life,
I'm instantly mesmerised,
Charmed by its magnitude,
A land to which I'll definitely return one day.

Autumn

The trees grow barer
as cold winds rape their branches.
Winter is stalking us.

Rivers and lakes grow
colder now as they turn to
ice – winter's diamonds.

The nights are cold again
the days are growing shorter,
hearths are ablaze.

A carpet of leaves cover
the green grass that was my lawn.
Thanks to autumn – again.

Winter

Winter rains pour down–
skies are bleak and foreboding,
thunder rumbles too.

The moon is shadowed and
wind bites us relentlessly
like a rabid dog.

Soft powdery snow
blankets the playground swings
and snowmen are born.

It rains endlessly.
Water drowns the once green lawn
now hidden deep down.

Spring

Birds are flying again;
their chirping echoes happiness.
Lakes and rivers thaw.

The days are warmer,
the clouds are fluffier,
hay fever wheezes in.

Children are playing
in the playground noisily,
their laughter a gift.

Clear blue skies are here
and so is the sun once more,
and so too, new lambs.

Summer

Lazy waves lap the shore
people swimming in the sea
sunburn in the breeze.

Warm, hazy days with
bees buzzing everywhere
and cows are grazing.

Hot winds and hot nights,
no relief anytime soon.
Sleepless nights prickle.

The days are hotter;
dry grass and broken glass –
a farmer's menace.

White Wings at Dawn

Morning comes too soon.
My alarm clock sings
then screeches and squawks,
telling me that tomorrow has begun.

Sunlight streams through
the window's lacy curtains
and into my sleepy eyes.
I roll over and feel its gentle warmth
on my shoulders and know only too well
that I can sleep no more.

Slowly, I wander out onto the porch
to meet the day and, sure enough,
there they are, those all too beautiful,
those all too noisy white wings at dawn,
filling the pale morning sky.

The Steely Bear

Like a bear in a cave, I hibernate,
just waiting for the warmer weather to awake,
and then I'll eat, eat, eat
with food left in my teeth
and on my face like a little child
but in the end nothing goes to waste
and should a finger get too close,
I might as well bite it too.

The Ghost of Emptiness

There is a ghost inside both of us,
a ghost that haunts the corridors of our hearts
and the doorway to our souls;
it is the same ghost that roams
through the corridors of our minds;
sadly it is a ghost that visits us all
and its name is
emptiness.

It roams through us like a gypsy,
with no particular place to be,
inside of you,
inside of me,
and until we are together,
as lovers should be –
unhampered and happy,
laughing and carefree –
with us it will sadly be.

Cold and Alone

The old man walks slowly through deserted streets
carpeted by soft white snow;
the wind blows so cruelly around him.
He is alone;
no children play in the freshly falling snow,
and no people walk there either.

His ragged jacket collar sits high around his neck,
and his scarf too, despite the holes;
his hat covers his balding head.
With his head hung low so the cold
snow and wind can't bite at him,
he trudges on like a homeless dog
looking for somewhere warmer to be.

'Why aren't there children playing in the snow?
Where have all the people gone?' he asks himself.
'Maybe it's too cold for them. Heaven only knows.'
Through a window he sees a family
huddled around a roaring fire,
the one thing he truly desires.

The little town would never be the same,
the steel mill closed down and many
local jobs were lost along with his faith
in himself and of finding work
in this place again.

He took his family north
in the hope of finding work
but it was on this trek that a car wreck
took away all that was important to him.

With his family now gone
he became a lonely hobo begging
and pleading, aching and needing for
somewhere to call home,
a place to soften the misery of loss,
a haven from the storm of loneliness and cold.

Somewhere In My Head

Somewhere in my head I'm alone
sitting on a deserted beach and my only companions
are the scattered boulders in front of me,
a full moon and a starless sky,
but something is missing and I don't know what it is
or who it is, but in time it will come to me.

The waves make a soft whooshing sound
as they gently kiss the shoreline and the rocks
off in the distance
before rolling back out to the open sea again
and still I'm lost here as nobody can find me;
I'm alone and still I can't remember what is missing,
can't remember who is missing, but it will come to me – maybe.

Somewhere in my head a piano is playing soft melodies.
I lie back in the cool sand and shut my eyes, unafraid of drowning –
here in the ocean, in the loneliness of my mind –
and still I can't remember what is missing,
still can't remember who is missing
and I don't know why this is so.

I hear a voice but it's not mine;
it calls to me from a distant place
somewhere in my head and it echoes
softly off my conscience, and for whatever reason
I'm not alarmed by its calling for I choose to be here,
lost in this place that I don't know,
a place somewhere in my head.

There it is again but this time it's louder,
not scared – not scared at all – just a little louder
in the hope of being heard, in the hope of reaching me.
It softly resonates as it draws nearer
but can it find me in this place that I am lost,
this place, somewhere in my head?

The once soft whooshing sound grows louder
as cool water tickles the soles of my feet.
I stir from my slumber but still the voice is calling out to me
in the hope of finding me, in the hope of bringing me home,
home from this place somewhere in my head.

Waterside Heaven

Here we are hidden away
from the prying eyes of others,
just you and me in this piece
of God's heaven on earth,
living and loving our lives away,
just you, me, the river and silence,
sweet beautiful silence,
and sweet, sacred love.

The Sound of Death

A scurrying gazelle,
A lioness driven by hunger.
In a cloud of dust death comes quick,
A whimpering last bleat,
A snarl of victory –
Hunger is sated.

Endless Night

He needed to sleep
and to be at peace within
without dreams
and haunting memories of days gone by;
his mind craved freedom,
he was burnt out– exhausted
without redemption.

Lying down with eyes shut tightly,
he could still see the violence,
still smell the death;
it was all too much and
needed to come to an end.

No longer could he face the horrors
of the battlefield;
the mutilations and corpses
he had seen and caused
had become a burden.
He was neither a robot nor humanoid –
a senseless cold killer,
he was only a young man sent to do
somebody else's dirty work and
it all must end.

He is home now
and still the dreams,
and the horrors
haunted him relentlessly every night
but tonight would be different.
Tonight he'd sleep an endless sleep
and should he not wake when they called,
they'd put pennies on his eyes
and mourn yet another passing.

Goodbye My Little Friend

For many years now you have filled my life with happiness,
with a companionship as only you can,
but now as you grow older and get slower
your bright little brown eyes don't see or shine so well any more;
your little legs that once scampered and scratched
as you ran up and down the hallway
ache with pain and you groan with every movement.

The time that I dreaded for so long has come at last,
the time for me to let you go even though it pains
me so but it must be done because I can't see you suffer,
I won't see you suffer because I love you.

I cradle you in my arms like a father would do for his child
and hold you tightly not wanting to let you go,
but I must, I must let you cross over the rainbow
into doggie heaven and be free of the suffering,
be free from the pain as though you were a puppy again.

The doctor gives you the needle that will release you
while you lie in my arms and I sob and snuffle as I say goodbye.
Your little heart beats no more but I can't bring myself to let
you go – not yet.
One last kiss upon your tiny head – one last cuddle.

Releasing my grip, they take you from me
before I leave the room heavy-hearted
so they can prepare you to be with me in ashes
and yet in all this sorrow and all this heartbreak comes joy
because at home there is a living memory
of you waiting for me who'll lick away the tears, lick away the pain,
the same pain that he feels and knows, for he is your son,
your little boy.

I sit cuddling him and cry yet some more as he licks my face
and in his own way he cuddles me, comforts me with his love –
his unconditional love.
He's my everlasting memory of you
and though the pain of my loss won't go away anytime soon,
I look into his bright little eyes and I see you –
my much-loved, my dearly departed little friend.

The Longest Trek

Side by side they walk
mother and calf, mother and calf
searching for that elusive golden pasture,
searching for that reviving cool, fresh water.

On and on they walk;
mile after mile there's nothing but dry, dead grass
and sand as dry as powder,
dry as their hides.
Trees are few and far between.

A calf weakens and begins to buckle
in the heat, the oppressive heat
that shows no mercy,
no caring, no caring at all.

The mother nudges the youngster
with her trunk but it's futile,
the little elephant can go no further –
all energy has been sapped from its little body
and yet the mother doesn't give up.

The rest of the herd keep moving,
eastward, in hope before their calves also
succumb to the heat
leaving the mother and her calf behind,
leaving the mother to watch her baby die

The mother gives one last glance downward
at her baby before walking away, knowing
there is nothing she can do but hope to catch
up with the herd and find what her dead baby needed most –
water in the dry Somali desert.

Don't Mourn for Me

To my beloved family,
mourn for me just a little,
as I'd rather that you celebrated my life
and smile with the fondest of memories
still young in your hearts.

Remember all of the beautiful things we did,
the wonderful times that we shared
and keep those forever in your hearts,
mourn me not for it's in your hearts
I'll forever be.

God has put out his hand and called to me
to join him in heaven
and so I must go
but I am not going alone,
for he has sent an escort of angels to guide
and walk with me upon that pillowy stairway
to where I'll stay,
till we are once again together, some day.

It's Never Easy

It never comes easy my friend, never
when somebody we know,
someone that we love, joins the angels
in heaven.

He was a father…your father
and a grandfather,
but most of all he was your friend
and in his own way;
know deep in your heart
that he always loved you till the end.

It's only normal to feel lost and distraught
so cry as much as you must
to relieve the hurt,
remember him in a shining light,
and with love in your heart.

Know this, our dear friend:
you'll always have us
waiting and willing to listen,
ready to give you a badly needed hug
when you need it most
to make things a little easier for you
and you a little happier as best we can
because we love you, Lisa our friend.

Into the Darkness

Day becomes night and the sky is dotted with
billions of stars – a sparkling blanket that
envelops, suffocates and scares us
with no way out, no means of escape.

Into the darkness we go upon conception
and there we stay until we are born;
into the darkness we are plunged
when we go to meet our maker
in a coffin so elaborately lined and warm.

Into the darkness they steal
their way on a journey of murder
and crime;
into the darkness they come,
the malevolent creatures of another world
less holier than ours searching for souls to steal,
lusting for blood and carnage
and should they fail, back
into the darkness they are plunged,
doomed for ever more,
back into a darkness more sinister,
more menacing than ours.

The Detour

In the cool shade of a crumbly old bridge
they hide in silence where the water is cool, murky and deep.
With lines cast, they wait and wait and wait, yet some more
for that one golden moment – for that all-important first tug,
telling them that the detour was worth it
and that school could wait, just a little while longer.

Two young boys just being boys
who had gone off fishing
instead of being in class
and listening
to the lessons of the day,
listening to what the teacher had to say.

The day grows older and hotter by the minute
as they begin to doze off thinking it
will never happen and that there will
be no fish on the line for them today
and then BAM – there it is – that all-important first tug,
that first bite that made the detour so sweet,
so worthwhile.

Was it cod or carp?
Time would tell as the youngster
reels it in because it fought like either.
A brownish-gold figure breaks the surface
fighting the fight of its life but the game is up,
and the boys have won, for old man cod is well
and truly on the line with no way out.
Dinner tonight will be oh so sweet
and as for the day away from school, secret never shared,
and the detour –
so worth it, this time round, at least.

Another New Chapter

The day we met was the start of another new chapter
in the book of life; our life.
The day we met was the start of another new chapter
in the book of love; our love.
Each and every day that passed saw us
grow closer, saw us growing stronger and tighter.
This chapter that had been waiting to be written,
for we were been born for this.
Me for you and you for me.
For on the walls of our hearts
the names had been tattooed,
and this is how it will always be,
for our love was so deep and so loyal,
passionate and powerful,
but above all our love will always be
indestructible and totally indisputable.

The Seed

Many, many years ago
a seed was sown
and it grew to be
the most beautiful of flowers
I have ever seen.

It was more beautiful than a protea
with a fragrance much sweeter
than the most beautiful of roses,
that flower is you,
my darling wife, Zelma.

You Are the Candle

You are the candle that lit the way for me
with the elegance of pearls;
you are as beautiful as the rose
and the sweet perfume it bestows,
And this, my darling, is why
I love you so.

One Candle

One candle glowing softly at night
was all it ever took to show our
love for one another.
Just a solitary candle
burning softly
while we made tender love.

Tell me, my love,
isn't it time we let that candle
burn once again to prove
that nothing has changed between us
like the soft glowing aura of
the candle or its soft warm wax
and indeed, the burning passion of our love.

Side By Side

Side by side we lie,
our minds entwined
as one at peace,
hearts beat in sync together,
our love is deep,
our love is forever.

Side by side we lie,
your head resting
on my shoulder,
fingers locked,
we are one,
this is our time,
this is our space
side by side,
side by side.

The Tears You Cry

The tears you cry fall softly on my shoulders
even though I am not there to cradle you,
nor does your sobbing fall on deaf ears,
my love, for I know and feel your anguish,
I know your desperation
and your frustration
for they are mine too.

Rest assured that we'll be together soon
in body just as we are in heart and soul,
this is our goal, our ambition.
Lean on me, angel, for I am your rock,
I am the lighthouse guiding you home,
so that we'll be together,
never to be torn apart.

Not Once

Not once have I forgotten what you mean to me,
not once have I forgotten what you have done for me;
you've been more than a lover to me,
you've been my friend, my confidante,
and that in itself means so much to me
(oh so much).

Not once have I doubted your sincerity
or your faithfulness because nobody can turn
your gaze from me;
it's always me that you come home to.
Not once have I had reason to question your
dedication to me as you're always there
when I need you most, making me laugh, making me smile
when my skies are dark and cold
and for all of this and so much more,
I believe in you –
and only you.

Only For You

Only for you do I write these words,
these verses,
and only because of you does my head
and my heart float here
in the clouds,
on the wings of angels,
but none as fair as you,
none, my angel,
and this why
I love you and only you.

Power of the Rose

It can woo you,
charm you,
its fragrance will even hypnotise you;
but tell me, angel,
can it love you, comfort you
like I would, like I can
when you're feeling down?
Will it support and caress you,
can it hold and love you
like I will, like I can?
Its beauty can come close but it
could and never will be you.

My Angel

Flap those beautiful
delicate wings, my angel,
as you come to me so softly.

Show me, show the world
your beauty and how radiantly you shine,
how beautifully you smile.

Show how beautiful you truly are
the keeper of my heart,
the keeper of my soul,
my friend, my lover –
my wife.

The Circle

For so long now I have waited to hear
from you and though it has been a
long painful wait, the waiting has been
worth it in the long run, but it should
never had been this way
and it never will be again.

The circle is complete,
for we are speaking once again
after fifteen long years.
The door to my heart was always wide open,
never slammed shut,
for now it has come to be that our relationship
as a father and his daughter has been reborn,
and now it will begin a new phase,
and the circle,
it will never to be broken again.

The Ruins

The ruins are all that's left
of a once strong and loving relationship
that has gone off the rails,
and into oblivion,
leaving behind nothing but an empty shell
of the person who is hurting the most,
the person who fought like crazy,
to save the sinking ship
and rebuild their shattered life,
hopefully find happiness in the arms of another,
to rebuild the ruins on a new foundation
a foundation of love and caring,
of truth and honesty.

A House Is Like a Baby

Planning to build a house
is like planning a pregnancy:
you've got to get it right.
You plan so that the house
is built and finished in good weather
and just like you plan the pregnancy,
you plan it so that the new arrival
comes in a season that is neither
too hot or too cold.

The time has come,
the house is built,
and baby's here, too –
welcome to the world of sleepless
nights and early-morning feeds.
You've chosen your furnishings,
colours and other special features
like you did for the baby
when you chose his clothes in the right combinations.
It's just like having twins when you think about it,
because that house is your baby too.

A Pleasant Place

The wooden tongue of an invisible serpent
reaches out into the murky depths
that's supported by rails,
and nailed to poles,
long ago, buried in this watery place.

Its boards, although rickety now,
are a platform for children to run
and dive from into the cool river water.
It's shaded and surrounded by evergreen
willow and peppercorn trees
while ugly black leeches lurk deep
waiting to suck their blood.

The children float on rubber tubes,
their young noses inhaling the musty
willowy breezes as they wave to passengers
on a passing river boat that makes its way slowly upstream
not to be seen again for another two days,
and when it does the kids will be waiting,
ready to bob up and down like corks on the lazy waves
that gently slap the nearby grassy banks.
This I know for sure, because I was one of them.

Candlelight Dancer

In a darkness broken only by
the glow of a solitary candle
she comes to me,
my candlelight dancer.

Dancing, dancing, dancing
is all that she does
to symphonies only she can hear.
Not a word does she speak
as she flitters to and fro
from side to side
avoiding the heat,
my candlelight dancer.

In the aura of the glow
she dances.
In the aura of the glow
she pirouettes and prances,
my tiny candlelight dancer.

My eyes grow heavy
and still she dances
untouched by the heat
of the flame;
hypnotising me is surely her game
so that I will sleep without
ever knowing her name,
my candlelight dancer.

Eric

Engaging and enthusiastic
Rich with knowledge for all of his years
Intellectual and inspiring
Charismatic – a champion of a bloke

Jude

Jovial, jaunty and justly
Understanding and sincere
Dedicated to what she does best
Enriched with a personality that can't be denied.

www.ingramcontent.com/pod-product-compliance
Lightning Source LLC
Chambersburg PA
CBHW062202100526
44589CB00014B/1923